THE LITTLE BOOK OF
CIGARS

By John Beilenson

Illustrated by Abigail Adams-Kelly

Designed by Arlene Greco

PETER PAUPER PRESS, INC.
WHITE PLAINS, NEW YORK

To my research associates:
James Dell'Orefice, Jack Laschever,
Jeff Preston, Peter Haabestad, and
Larry and Esther Beilenson

Copyright © 1997
Peter Pauper Press, Inc.
202 Mamaroneck Avenue
White Plains, NY 10601
All rights reserved
ISBN 0-88088-062-7
Printed in China
7 6 5 4 3 2 1

CONTENTS

A Good Smoke: An Introduction

Sigmund Freud once said that a cigar is just a cigar, but cigar smoking today is also about elegance, simplicity, and ease. The slow, cultivated ritual of choosing, cutting, and lighting a premium cigar provides a tranquil pause in any harried day. The close contact with an artifact that must pass through the careful hands of more than 100 people from harvest to packing celebrates an increasingly rare kind of craftsmanship. And the exhalation of thick blue clouds of cigar smoke yields a subtle and restorative pleasure.

Socially, cigar smoking encourages us to seek out others—

and is best enjoyed in the company of friends or family. Traditionally shared to celebrate a new birth or a promotion, cigars also create momentary "celebrations" out of simple contact with friends or family. Cigars heighten the timeless, and often forgotten, joy of sitting down in a comfortable chair and just talking. Cigars also enhance unhurried time alone when one can simply savor the moment. Zino Davidoff, the founder of the Davidoff cigar empire, captured this sentiment nicely. Cigar smoking, he wrote, not only celebrates both sublime and precious occasions, but "like the smoke that rises from the gray ash, fleeting . . . unforgettable" moments, as well.

J. B.

SMOKING! CIGARS YESTERDAY AND TODAY

*S*ome claim that the word *cigar* (or in Spanish *cigarro*) derives from the Spanish *cigaral* or *cicada.* The actual derivation, however, is from the Mayan words *ciq-sigan* meaning "smoking," and *sikar* meaning "to smoke." Early cigars were wrapped in palm or maize leaves, but the cigar as we know it—tobacco leaf wrapped in tobacco leaf—was first created in Seville in 17th century Spain.

The origin of the cigar band, according to legend, dates to the regal fingers of Russia's Catherine the Great, more than two centuries ago. It is said that she ordered her cigars cloaked in silk to protect her hands from tobacco stains. In imitation of the Queen, silk cigar bands were adopted; the cigar band, now made of a colorful though more modest paper, was born.

Several U.S. Presidents have known the pleasure of a good cigar. John Adams and John Quincy Adams were partial to cigars, as was James Madison, the first President to smoke in the White House after it was rebuilt from ashes following the War of 1812. Andrew Jackson and his wife smoked cigars together. General and later President Ulysses S. Grant was said to smoke 10 stogies a day during his successful Civil War campaign. In the early part of the 20th century, Warren Harding, Calvin Coolidge, and Herbert Hoover all indulged in the Presidential cigar habit.

While President Bill Clinton has been seen with a cigar on the golf course from time to time, the last regular cigar smoker in the Oval Office was John F. Kennedy. Just prior to signing the embargo on all Cuban products entering the United States in 1961, he entreated his press secretary Pierre Salinger to gather as many H. Upmann petit coronas—Kennedy's favorites—as he could find. Salinger collected 1,100 before Kennedy signed the decree. In 1996, JFK's (empty) humidor fetched a record $575,000 at Sotheby's auction of the estate of Jacqueline Kennedy Onassis.

Perhaps the most visually memorable cigar-smoking political figure was Winston Churchill, who led England throughout World War II with a thick cigar constantly between his teeth. It is estimated that Churchill smoked more than 250,000 cigars during his lifetime.

Cigar smoking and great literature have often gone hand in hand. William Thackeray punctuated each writing day with several cigars. Mark Twain smoked constantly (about three cigars an hour, according to his own reckoning) and once wrote famously, "If I cannot smoke in heaven, then I shall not go." Nobel prize-winning poet and

writer Rudyard Kipling penned the English language's most famous "cigar" poem about a man who chooses cigars over his fiancée, saying, "A woman is only a woman, but a good cigar is a smoke." Clear-headed thinkers might perhaps consider Kipling's position extreme.

Great women writers including Gertrude Stein, Amy Lowell, and Colette also have extolled the virtues of the cigar. Lucile Aurore Dupin Dudevant, better known as George Sand, smoked as many as seven cigars a day. She once said, "A cigar numbs sorrow and fills the solitary hours with a million gracious images."

Before the rise of the smoking club or *divan*, a privileged domain of Victorian English gentlemen, men and women smoked in equal numbers, both in the Old World and the New. Traveling in Costa Rica during the early part of the 18th century, John Cockburn observed, "These gentlemen gave us some seegars . . . these are leaves of tobacco rolled up in such a manner that they serve both for a pipe and for tobacco itself. These the ladies, as well as the gentlemen, are very fond of smoking."

Entertainers—and particularly comedians—have always had a soft spot for the cigar. Cigars

figured prominently in several Charlie Chaplin films. W. C. Fields, Groucho Marx, and Jimmy Durante were well-known smokers, and more recently Bill Cosby, Chevy Chase, and David Letterman have been known to light up.

Perhaps the most famous cigar-smoking funny man was George Burns. On stage, he smoked machine-made cigars (El Producto Queens) because they stayed lit longer than hand-rolled ones. As he said at 98, two years before he died, "If I'd have taken my doctor's advice and quit smoking when he advised me to, I wouldn't have lived to go to his funeral."

In Hollywood, the cigar currently has a high profile. Arnold

Schwarzenegger, Demi Moore, Danny DeVito, Jack Nicholson, Robert De Niro, Whoopi Goldberg, Gregory Hines, Harvey Keitel, Tom Selleck, Linda Evangelista, and the late Raul Julia have all proudly made their passion for fine cigars public knowledge.

We are in the middle of a cigar boom, in particular a premium cigar boom. In 1992, the United States imported only 99 million handmade cigars. By 1996, this had risen to more than 275 million cigars, including an estimated 6 million that were made in Cuba, purchased abroad, and smuggled into the States.

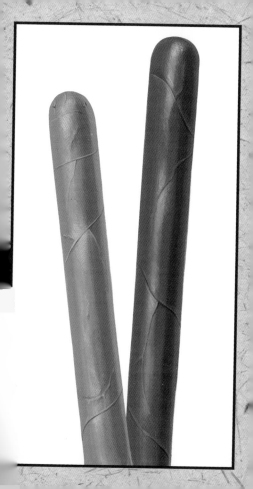

With this surge in demand for imported (generally handmade) cigars, suppliers have strained to keep pace. From planting to packing, it takes between two and three years to create a box of premium cigars. Not surprisingly, prices have skyrocketed during the past several years. Vintage cigars are attracting similar interest. In 1996, Peter de Savary of the Carnegie Club at Scotland's Skibo Castle paid a whopping $28,570 at a Christie's auction for 163 of the world's oldest Havana cigars, dating back to the late 1850s.

While we are enjoying a cigar renaissance now, the Golden Age of the American cigar was surely the half-century between

1870 and 1920, when American firms produced more than 1.5 million brands of cigars, and manufactured 250 billion cigars. In 1900, it was estimated that four out of five men (as well as a healthy percentage of women) smoked cigars. Nearly 150,000 cigar factories dotted the country, rolling domestic and imported tobacco into 3,500 shapes and sizes. The word "stogie" (a derivative of Conestoga) was coined during this era. (This Pennsylvania town was known not only for its cigar production, but also for constructing the covered wagons that brought American settlers west.) This cigar smoking boom came to a halt in a single decade—the 1920s—as cheap, machine-produced cigarettes became widely available and exceedingly popular.

CHOOSING A CIGAR

*W*alking into a cigar store with its myriad offerings can be daunting. However, your local tobacconist should provide you with a little gentle guidance and hasten your cigar education. Publications such as *Cigar Aficionado, Smoke,* and others provide thorough descriptions of particular brands and sizes. The important thing—especially for the novice—is not to find and buy the most expensive cigars or to develop a 400-word vocabulary describing their taste, but rather to try a selection of cigars ("singles," as they are called in the trade). Find ones that deliver satisfaction time and again before investing in a full box of smokes. As Joel Sherman, son of legendary cigar merchant Nat Sherman, has written, "When it comes to choosing the right cigar, there's only one expert, and that's you!"

The Global Cigar

First, consider the cigar's country of origin. Knowing where the cigar comes from can give you a hint of what the cigar is like. Speaking generally of course, cigars from the United States or the Philippines tend to be quite mild. Jamaican and Dominican cigars are generally lighter tasting. Hondurans are more full-bodied and spicy; Nicaraguans, medium-bodied and sweet; Brazilians, heavier and spicy; Cubans—again speaking generally—are medium- to full-bodied and can be almost chocolatey. Mexican cigars, however, vary widely.

Brand Loyalty

Beyond the cigar's birthplace, its brand often speaks volumes. Each brand offers several different sizes and shapes, but in general (and of course there are significant exceptions) the quality and taste of a successful brand will be consistent. For example, most Macanudos are light and spicy, most Punches more full-bodied and nutty.

You Can *Judge* a Cigar by Its Wrapper

The wrapper—the thin, outermost layer of the cigar—has a disproportionate effect on its taste. The lighter the color of the cigar's wrapper, the lighter the smoke. Similarly, the darker the wrapper, the more intense the cigar's flavor. Wrapper colors vary from *candela* or *claro claro* (almost greenish) to *oscuro* (a very dark, black coffee color). A well-made cigar should have a fine-veined wrapper with no nicks or cuts that may lead to an uneven burn. Any cigar with a cracked or broken wrapper should be rejected. You should inspect a cigar or box of cigars before purchasing them. Pinch cigars lightly to ensure that they are moist and well-constructed. Avoid rolling them roughly between your fingers or aggressively sniffing them, since over-handling can cause damage that makes cigars unsaleable.

Size Matters

The final consideration in choosing a cigar is its size. A cigar's length is usually from four inches to eight inches, although some special smokes

are as long as 18 inches. The cigar's girth or ring gauge is signified in increments of 1/64". A ring gauge of 32 indicates a cigar is 1/2 (32/64) inch in diameter. A ring gauge of 50 reflects a cigar 50/64" in diameter. The longer and thicker the cigar, the cooler its smoke. Larger cigars also allow the roller to use a greater variety of tobacco, enhancing the cigar's flavor. Larger cigars tend to be more expensive, so cigar manufacturers use their finest wrapper leaves and allow only their most experienced rollers to construct them. Not surprisingly, they tend to be better made.

If the Cigar Fits . . .
Of course, whatever cigar you choose, you will know what you think about one pretty soon after

you start smoking it. Lit, a cigar should be a pleasure to behold. It should look right and feel right in your hands. It should resonate with your spirit and personality. Its taste should be pleasant and appropriate to the time of day and the circumstances in which it is smoked. A large, full-bodied cigar may be perfect after an elegant dinner. But if you have only a brief respite before returning to your smoke-free workplace, you might try something smaller and lighter.

Storing Your Cigars

When purchasing cigars, remember that they are a natural, perishable product and must be stored appropriately at 70° Fahrenheit and 70% humidity. The lower humidity of most homes and offices will dry out a cigar in an hour or two. Higher temperatures and humidity encourage mold and the larvae of tobacco beetles. A box or cellophane wrapper may preserve a cigar for a few days. A sealed tube may protect it longer. If you do not plan on smoking your purchases immediately, however, you should invest in a humidor. These can be found in an array of sizes. Generally, humidors are well-sealed wooden boxes lined with Spanish cedar, humidified with a sponge-like mechanism called a humistat or credo, and the humidity measured by a hygrometer or humidity gauge. Makeshift humidors, while decidedly less elegant, can be made from Tupperware, a tall Mason jar, or even a plastic picnic cooler, with a humistat and hygrometer placed inside.

ENJOYING A GOOD CIGAR

*E*njoying a good cigar takes time. The slow ritual of cutting and lighting a cigar before smoking serves to focus attention away from stress or worry to the experience at hand. How exactly to conduct this "ritual" is the matter of some debate and personal preference, but its conduct does have an impact on the quality of your smoke.

The Kindest Cut

You must first cut the head—that is, the closed end—of the cigar. This will allow you to draw on the cigar smoothly and easily. Make a quick, clean cut, no more than 1/4" from the end. This preserves the integrity of the cigar's cap, a piece of wrapper tobacco cut and placed specifically to close the cigar. If you slice the entire cap off, pieces of the cigar's filler may flake into your mouth while smoking. Worse, the cigar may unravel. Single-bladed, hand-sized guillotines available at the local tobacconist are perfectly serviceable, though more expensive double-bladed models will provide a cleaner, more consistent result.

Other options include cigar scissors, often made of silver or brass. These are beautiful to look at, but require some skill to use and are difficult to carry. Cigar punches extract a narrow wedge or circle at the head, and some aficionados swear by them. Others (especially those who hold a cigar with their teeth) complain that the wedge may cause the end of the cigar to collapse or that the smallish opening makes for hotter smoke on the tongue. In general, avoid biting the end of a fine cigar (unless you find yourself in the wilderness or on the 10th tee without a cutting device). Your incisors may rip the cap, and damage the cigar.

Further Preparations

Once the cigar is cut, do not run a flame down the cigar or lick it from end to end. These practices date to a time near the turn of the last century when cigars were often ill-made, and manufacturers employed foul vegetable gums to keep the wrapper from unraveling. Licking ensured that a cigar remained bound while smoking. The flame burned off the gums before smoking. Neither technique is necessary today.

Similarly, in days gone by, the cigar band often helped to keep the cigar intact. Removing the band was risky business. Today, it is a matter of taste. In England, for example, leaving the band on is considered ostentatious. In the United States, there is no hard and fast tradition. If you do want to remove the band, however, it is probably wise to wait until the heat of the cigar loosens it slightly so it can slip off with no ill effects to the wrapper.

Lighting Up

Wooden matches or butane lighters are preferred for lighting a cigar. Paper matches do not burn long enough, and gas lighters allow the scent of kerosene to invade the cigar. Some traditionalists favor cedar spills (strips of cedar broken off

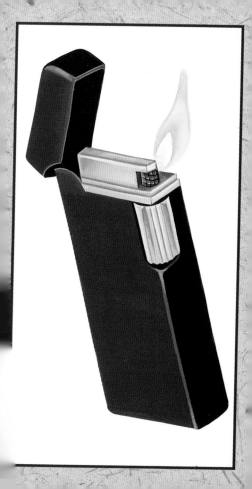

the insides of cigar boxes), which are aromatic, but may also flame a bit uncontrollably. Whichever method you prefer, hold the foot or open end of the cigar above the flame at a 30-40° angle and rotate the cigar slowly until the cigar is warm, and the entire rim is lit. Then, place the cigar in your mouth and puff gently, pulling the flame across the foot. Avoid drawing on the cigar with the foot placed in the heart of the flame. This may overheat the cigar, and scorched tobacco loses some of its complex flavor. With the foot fully lit, blow lightly on it or swirl the cigar gently to encourage the ember to spread. Take time to enjoy the initial light swirls of burning tobacco. Before puffing heartily on the cigar, blow out through the cigar to ensure that any carbon or other impurities developed during lighting are not sucked through the cigar to taint the rest of your smoke.

Other Considerations

Do not inhale cigar smoke; it is quite strong and will induce choking and nausea. Puff gently and take the smoke in, allow it to coat the inside of your mouth, and then blow it out. As you smoke, the ash of a well-rolled cigar will grow to some length. Resist the temptation to knock it right off, as this ash protects the ember and encourages the cigar to burn evenly. Most well-aged cigar tobacco will produce a grey or whitish-grey ash with a thin carbon ring where the ash meets the unburned portion of the cigar. A blacker ash often reflects an overly moist cigar.

Take your time while smoking. Sit back and relax. Consider the cigar and its characteristics as it burns or simply enjoy the smoke as it wafts around your conversation. If your cigar happens to go out, not to worry. Simply knock off the ash, blow through the cigar to clear it of any stale smoke, and re-light the cigar. To avoid unpleasant odors (and the wrath of anyone you may be sharing your living quarters with), dispose of cigar butts and ashes soon after smoking.

FROM SEED TO SALE: PRODUCING A PREMIUM CIGAR

*G*reat tobacco is grown in the Dominican Republic, Honduras, Jamaica, Nicaragua, and even Connecticut, though most still acknowledge that Cuban tobacco is the finest in the world. Generally cultivated on small plots in the Vuelta Abajo area of the western province of Pinar del Rio, this tobacco flourishes in the region's reddish sandy loam. But whether in Cuba or in other parts of the world, the production of premium handmade cigars is a careful and time-consuming process.

Special plants called *corojos*, which are grown beneath gauze sheets, produce the thin, paper-smooth leaves used in wrappers of fine quality, hand-made cigars. Each plant can yield as many as 32 wrappers. The tobacco used to produce the rest of the cigar (the binder and filler) is grown in the full sun. The filler of larger high quality cigars is generally blended from the aromatic top or *ligero* leaves of the plant, the lighter middle or *seco* leaves, and the coarse bottom or *volado* leaves, which are used for bulk and for their burning qualities.

Once harvested, all tobacco leaves must be cured, stacked and fermented, cooled, and sorted according to color, size and texture, fermented a second time, baled, and only then shipped to the tobacco factory for rolling. This extensive process reduces the levels of acidity, tar, and nicotine in the leaves, making cigar tobacco much more flavorful than cigarette tobacco.

At the cigar factory, expert rollers transform the well-aged tobacco leaves into handmade cigars. These rollers or *torcedores* spend as many as 10 years in training before earning the right to create a brand's premium smokes. The *torcedor* begins the process by laying two to four filler leaves end to end, then crimps them together into two halves that resemble closed fans. These are called the "bunch." The leaves must be evenly distributed to ensure a proper draw. The bunch is then wrapped in a binder leaf, placed in a wooden cigar mold, and shaped further by a bunch press.

Any surplus leaf is trimmed off. The *torcedor* then fashions a wrapper leaf to size and carefully rolls it around the bunch. A dab of colorless and odorless vegetable gum secures the wrapper. The cap, a small coin-sized patch of tobacco, is affixed to the head of the cigar to help secure the wrapper. Finally, the open end or foot is created with a quick decisive cut. A talented *torcedor* can make as many as 200 medium-sized cigars in a day, though 60-90 is the average for larger, more expensive sizes.

After rolling, cigars are fumigated against potential pests, and some of each roller's output is tested for quality. Tasters or *catadores* work in the morning, sipping sugarless tea between cigars to cleanse their palates.

After passing inspection, batches of cigars are placed in cooling cabinets to remove any excess moisture and to stop additional fermentation. When ready, cigars are separated into different color grades—65 in all. Finally, cigars of a similar grade are gathered, banded, placed in a box, and sealed, ensuring that they arrive at your local tobacconist fresh and ready to enjoy.

THE ART
OF THE CIGAR

*T*he primary appeal of cigars is in their smoking, but thanks to a long tradition of point-of-purchase advertising, we can also enjoy the esthetic allure of cigar bands and cigar box labels.

While silk bands date to the days of Catherine the Great, paper cigar bands were first used commercially during the 1830s to identify cigars as real Cubans, rather than the cheap knock-offs then being passed off as the real thing in Europe. When the bulk of the world's cigar production moved to the United States during the late 19th century, colorful bands were used to differentiate the hundreds of cigar brands offered for sale. Collecting these bands became something of a fashion, especially after the American Cigar Company began offering premiums in exchange for collected bands of their cigars. For 600 bands, for example, you could receive a subscription to *Scientific American* magazine; for 179,950, you could acquire a baby grand piano. The derogatory term *guttersnipe* derived from the practice of poor children scrounging city streets in search of these bands and the gifts their redemption brought. Turn-of-the-century bands and ashtrays are now collectors' items.

The beautiful 12-colored lithograph labels used on cigar boxes have also attracted collectors' interest. Originally, cigars were bundled in pigs' bladders, often with a sprig of vanilla to improve the scent of the package. Boxing cigars (in

the United States at least) began in earnest as a result of the Revenue Act of 1864, which sought to regulate and tax cigar production to help pay for the Civil War. This legislation ensured that all imported and domestic cigars were packed in branded boxes containing 25, 50, 100, or 250 cigars. Later in the century, as the cigar industry heated up, labels displayed on the inside of these boxes were used to attract the attention of cigar shoppers. Custom labels were developed for orders of as small as 10 boxes. They depicted everything from dogs and baseball players to gambling scenes and nudes. Thousands of new brands (and labels) were developed each year, supporting large commercial printers in lower Manhattan, Elmira, New York, and other regional centers of cigar production. In the 1920s, however, as cigarettes came into vogue (along with photoengraving and four-color printing presses), the variety of these litho cigar labels declined precipitately. Today, cigar labels, like cigar bands, are collectibles.

While cigar bands and labels cannot be considered "high art," they are examples of commercial artisanship and advertising, beautiful artifacts of the first golden era of cigar production in the United States.

Today, in a new golden age of the cigar, we can practice the great pleasure of cigar smoking, armed with a knowledge of the history, manufacture, quality, variety, and, yes, the high art of cigars and cigar smoking. It's time to sit back, light up, and enjoy.

CIGAR TERMS: A SELECTED GLOSSARY

Wrappers

A cigar's wrapper is responsible for most of a cigar's taste and all of its appearance. The color of a cigar's wrapper, therefore, can provide an important clue to the type of smoke you can expect.

Candela or Claro Claro. A green shade of wrapper created through heat-curing and providing a very mild taste, this leaf may also be called A.M.S. (American Market Selection) as it used to be very popular in the States.

Claro. A yellowish tan leaf with a neutral, unassuming flavor.

Colorado Claro. A light brown leaf (between the Colorado and Claro) with a pleasant mild taste.

Colorado. Reddish brown to brown, this rich-flavored wrapper is sometimes called E.M.S (English Market Selection) because of its popularity in Britain.

Colorado Maduro. A *cafe au lait* color, this wrapper has a medium strength taste.

Maduro. Literally "ripe," a maduro is a chocolate brown colored wrapper with a rich full flavor. It is also known as S.M.S. or Spanish Market Selection.

Oscuro. This almost black wrapper is quite rare and is generally found only on Brazilian cigars.

Sizes and Shapes

Most cigars have straight sides. Some, however, are shaped and are often referred to as *figurados*. The lengths and ring sizes listed below are the traditional dimensions of a particular size or shape, though actual cigars may vary.

Straight-Sided Cigars

Name	Length	Ring Size
Churchill	7"	48
Corona	5-1/2"	42-44
Corona Gorda	5-5/8"	46
Double Corona	7-1/2-8"	49-52
Lonsdale	6-1/4"	42-44

Panatela	5-7-1/2"	34-38
Petit Corona	4-1/2"	40-42
Robusto	5-5-1/2"	50

Shaped Cigars

Bellicoso   5-1/2"   52
   Originally a short pyramid,
   it is now often a corona or
   corona gorda with a
   tapered head.

Culebra   5-6"   3 x 38
   Literally "snake," the
   culebra is actually three
   panatelas braided and
   banded together. Each is
   smoked separately.

Diadema   8"+   60+

> Closed on both ends, this massive torpedo-shaped cigar broadens significantly from head to foot.

Perfecto   4-1/2-9"   38-48

> Also closed at both ends with a rounded head, this cigar is shaped with a bulge in the middle.

**Pyramid/
Torpedo**   6-7"   40/52-54

> While both boast a tapered head, the pyramid differs from a torpedo in that the pyramid's foot (or smoking end) is cut, while the foot of the torpedo is closed.

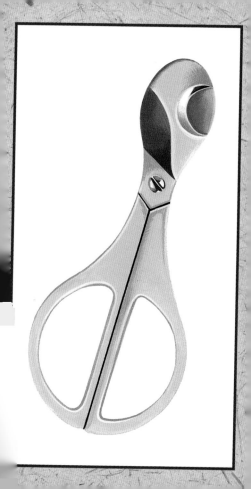

Parts of the Cigar

Head The end of the cigar you hold in your mouth.

Foot The end of the cigar you light.

Cap Small piece of tobacco that covers the head and ensures the integrity of the wrapper when the cigar is cut.

Wrapper Thin, elastic leaf that covers a cigar.

Binder   The leaf under the
           wrapper that holds
           the filler in place
           and ensures an
           even burn.

Filler   The tobacco leaves
           that make up the
           bulk of the "inside"
           of a cigar. In hand-
           made cigars, the
           filler is folded like
           a fan. In machine-
           made cigars, it is
           often ground like a
           cigarette. There are
           three types of filler
           leaf:

Ligero   Aromatic top leaves of the tobacco plant used for flavor.

Seco   Lighter, middle leaves of the plant, used mostly for bulk.

Volado   Coarser bottom leaves used for bulk and slow burning qualities.